Hi 🙂

Thought you might enjoy some of the tastes of the islands that are gentle on the pocket book.

This is a "melting pot" of many cultures + fusion of cuisines.

Let me know what you think.

Take care,
Carly

Little
Hawaiian
Noodle
Cookbook

Compiled by Joanne Fujita

MUTUAL PUBLISHING

ISBN 1-56647-689-5
Library of Congress Catalog Card Number: 2004112030

Photographs © Douglas Peebles

Design by Emily R. Lee

First Printing October 2004
1 2 3 4 5 6 7 8 9

Mutual Publishing, LLC
1215 Center Street, Suite 210
Honolulu, Hawai'i 96816
Ph: 808-732-1709 / Fax: 808-734-4094
e-mail: mutual@mutualpublishing.com
www.mutualpublishing.com

Printed in Korea

TABLE OF CONTENTS

Soba and Somen

Pasta

Noodle Glossary

INTRODUCTION

Hawai'i has been described as a melting pot of Asian cultures, and the best culinary reflection of this fact may well be in the wide variety of noodle dishes her residents enjoy. Traditional Hawaiian food never included noodles, but now, noodles count among the most popular snacks and light meals in the Islands.

Chinese Egg Noodles

The Chinese brought egg noodles, and with them, the beloved Saimin was created, a noodle soup unique to Hawai'i. Saimin is so ubiquitous as an instant noodle dish or saimin stand snack; local people never make this dish from scratch. However, Fried Saimin is a classic bachelor's meal. A simple recipe for this is included in this book. Chinese egg noodles find their way into stir-fries, soups and salads, and are the first thing locals think of when they hear "noodles".

Bean Thread Noodles

The Chinese also brought bean thread noodles, called "long rice" in Hawai'i. Perhaps the only noodle dish one will find at a traditional Hawaiian lū'au is Chicken Long Rice, as it has been a favorite for so long it can count as a Hawai'i classic. But this is just one of the many uses of "long rice": local concoctions with the slithery translucent noodles reflect many cultural influences. Included in this book is the Thai favorite Yum Woon Sen or Thai Long Rice Salad, studded with shrimp and pork and spiked with a lively dressing of lime juice and chilies. The Japanese influence is strong in the Abalone Long Rice Salad, which enlivens abalone and cucumbers with a rice vinegar marinade. Popular Filipino Pancit Miki pairs long rice with thick wheat noodles in a stew-like dish flavored with achiote seeds. Long rice noodles, which soak up the flavors of anything cooked with it, have soaked up a variety of cultures as well!

Rice Stick Noodles

In more recent years, the foods of Southeast Asia have become very popular, and the Thai and Vietnamese noodle of choice is the rice stick noodle. Restaurants selling the scrumptious Vietnamese beef noodle soup Pho have become just as numerous as saimin stands. Pad Thai, an internationally loved Thai noodle stir-fry, is also a big favorite in Hawai'i. The recipe in this book has been adapted from a genuine Bangkok formula that uses tamarind pulp. Rice stick noodles may also by deep-fried, making them delicately puffy and crisp. They make a very special chicken salad as you will see if you try the Crispy Chinese Chicken Salad.

Soba and Somen Noodles

Japan's culinary influence is evident in the consumption of soba (buckwheat) and somen (very thin white wheat noodles). These light, refreshing noodles have the advantage of being satisfying without any addition of fat—whether served chilled or hot. Served in a clean-tasting broth, they are perfect for hot weather. Hawai'i's delicate crimson snapper, the 'ōpakapaka, makes an appearance in 'Ōpakapaka with Somen Noodles- a dish fit for the finest palates.

Pasta

Finally, pasta has taken on a local accent too—and you'll see elegant creations by celebrity chef Roy Yamaguchi as well as local home cooking classics to see Hawai'i's take on the Italian noodle.

Enjoy!

CHINESE EGG NOODLES

Perhaps the most popular type of Asian noodle in local households, the versatile egg noodle is made into refreshing cold salads, fried like Chow Mein or Yakisoba, or put in delicious soups such as the Duck Noodle Soup. In this chapter, you will discover Toasted Noodles formed in a cake and an easy baked version of Chow Mein.

Chinese egg noodles are sold both fresh and dried. Recipes are for fresh noodles unless otherwise stated.

Cold Chinese Noodles with Cucumber

Serves 2

This dish is popular beach food in Japan. It's popular in Hawai'i, too, and you'll be able to buy yakisoba noodles and sauce at any Hawai'i supermarket.

Sauce
2 tablespoons Asian sesame oil
1 tablespoon soy sauce
1 tablespoon rice vinegar
1/4 teaspoon sugar
1/4 teaspoon salt, or to taste
1/8 teaspoon chili pepper flakes (optional)

6 ounces Chinese egg noodles, capellini or somen noodles
1/2 cucumber, seeds removed, cut into thin slices 1-1/2-inch
    long and 1/4-inch wide, about 1 cup
1 scallion (green onion) minced, or 1 tablespoon minced
    fresh coriander
1-1/2 teaspoons sesame seeds, toasted lightly and cooled

In a small bowl stir together sauce ingredients until sugar and salt are dissolved.

In a large saucepan in salted boiling water cook noodles until tender and drain in a colander. Rinse noodles under cold water until cool, and mix together with ice cubes and chill until noodles are cold. Remove ice cubes and drain noodles well.

In a large bowl, toss noodles with sauce, cucumber and scallion or coriander until combined well and divide between 2 plates. Sprinkle noodles with sesame seeds.

Peanut Noodle Salad

Serves 2

Noodle Salad

8 ounces (1/2 pound) Chinese egg noodles or linguine
1 teaspoon sesame oil
5 carrots, peeled and grated
2 cucumbers, seeded, halved lengthwise, shredded and
   squeezed dry
2 cups bean sprouts, rinsed and drained
1 red bell pepper, cored, seeded and cut into thin strings
2 cups cooked chicken, cut or hand shredded into thin strings
   OR 2 cups fried tofu, sliced into thin strips, placed in a
   colander, blanched with boiling water and drained
1-1/2 tablespoons minced scallion (green onion)
Peanut Dressing (see recipe on next page)

Boil noodles until just tender, drain in a colander and rinse
with cold water until cool. Drain well. Toss 1 teaspoon
sesame oil with the noodles so noodles keep separated.
Arrange noodles in a large serving bowl.

Arrange vegetables and chicken or tofu decoratively over the
noodles and sprinkle the scallions on top.

Serve at room temperature or chilled, with the Peanut Dressing.

Peanut Dressing
1-1/2 inch piece fresh ginger, peeled and sliced in half
8 cloves garlic, peeled
1 teaspoon chili paste, or more to taste
1/2 cup smooth peanut butter
1/4 cup soy sauce
3-1/2 tablespoons sugar
3-1/2 tablespoons Chinese black vinegar or rice vinegar
3 tablespoons Asian sesame oil
5 tablespoons chicken broth or water

In a food processor fitted with a metal blade or in a blender, finely chop the ginger and garlic. Add the remaining ingredients in the order listed and process until smooth. The dressing should be the consistency of heavy cream. If it is too thick, add more water or chicken broth; if too thin, add more peanut butter. The dressing will keep in the refrigerator for 2 to 3 weeks if kept in a covered container.

Cha Chiang Mein
Peking Noodles

Serves 4

1 pound fresh Chinese egg noodles
2 cups bean sprouts
2 cups won bok (Chinese cabbage)
1/2 cup cooked fresh or defrosted frozen peas
2 teaspoons salt
1 tablespoon vegetable oil
2 tablespoons yellow bean sauce
1 cup ground pork
2 teaspoons sugar
1/2 pound pork, sliced
4 cups water

Remove stringy roots from bean sprouts. Place in colander and pour boiling water over to blanch. Drain well and set aside.

Slice the cabbage. Place sliced pork in 4 cups of boiling water and simmer for 1 hour. Add 1 teaspoon salt. Boil cabbage in the pork stock just until tender. Remove cabbage from stock and set aside.

Mash the yellow bean sauce and place in large sieve. Set sieve over a bowl and slowly pour in 1/2 cup of water, stirring constantly and forcing bean sauce through sieve. Discard solids remaining in sieve. In 1 tablespoon oil, fry the ground pork, stirring until it is cooked. Add the sieved bean sauce and sugar and stir until mixture boils.

Just before serving, boil noodles for 4 minutes in a large pot of boiling water with 3 teaspoons salt. Drain well. Divide noodles among 4 bowls. Serve bean sprouts, cabbage, ground pork and peas in separate bowls. Have each person place desired amount of each condiment on his/her noodles.

Easy Fried Saimin

Serves 6

This is as authentically local Hawaiian as it gets. You will need to purchase instant saimin to make this, so it's unlikely you'll be able to make this on the Mainland. This recipe is included just for fun.

2 packages instant saimin
2 eggs
1/4 stick kamaboko (fish cake)
1/2 can Spam® or other luncheon meat or 1/2 cup char siu
    barbecued pork, cut in slivers
Soup base from 1 package of saimin
Soy sauce, to taste
2 green onions, chopped
Cooking oil

Boil the noodles from the instant saimin packages until done but still firm. Drain noodles in colander. Beat the eggs to combine yolks and whites and fry lightly. Set eggs aside. Fry the luncheon meat (if using) with a small amount of oil and stir in noodles and kamaboko. Fry noodles until crisp. Sprinkle soup base over noodles and mix in. Season noodles with soy sauce. Stir in scrambled eggs and green onions.

Yakisoba
Japanese Fried Noodles
Serves 6

This dish is popular beach food in Japan. It's popular in Hawai'i, too, and you'll be able to buy yakisoba noodles and sauce at any Hawai'i supermarket.

1/4 pound pork, cut into thin slices 1/2 inch by 1-1/2 inches
1 teaspoon vegetable oil
1/2 small onion, chopped
1 small carrot, julienned
1/4 of a small cabbage, julienned
3 single serving packages yakisoba noodles
        (or 3/4 pound Chinese egg noodles)
1/2 cup water
1/3 cup bottled yakisoba sauce
        OR seasoning packets that came with yakisoba noodles
        OR Homemade Yakisoba Sauce (see next page)
Beni-Shoga (slivered red ginger), optional
Ao Nori (dried green seaweed), optional

Heat oil in a large enough frying pan to accommodate noodles, and sauté pork until no longer pink. Add vegetables, starting with the onions, and stir-fry until they are limp.

continued on next page

Add noodles to pan, and stir well to separate. Add 1/2 cup of water and cover pan with lid. Allow to steam for about a minute. Remove lid, raise heat to medium-high and add yakisoba sauce or seasoning. Stir and toss noodles to coat well with sauce and fry for a few minutes. The water should mostly evaporate out, leaving the noodles and vegetables fairly dry. Garnish with a teaspoon of Beni-Shoga and a sprinkling of Ao Nori for each serving.

Homemade Yakisoba Sauce
1-1/2 tablespoons ketchup
3 tablespoons Worcestershire sauce
1/2 tablespoon soy sauce

Combine in a bowl.

Duck Noodle Soup

Serves 4

3-3/4 cups well-seasoned chicken stock
1/4 cup rice wine or sherry
1 2-inch chunk ginger, crushed
3 stalks green onions, crushed
1/8 teaspoon five spice powder

1 pound fresh or 11 ounces dried Chinese egg noodles

3/4 pound Chinese roast duck (store-bought is fine),
    cut into pieces
1/4 pound Chinese cabbage or bok choy, shredded
2 tablespoons soy sauce
Sesame oil

Add wine, ginger, green onions and five spice powder to chicken stock and bring to a boil. Reduce the heat and let remain at the simmering point.

Cook the noodles in plentiful salted water until al dente, then drain and divide between 4 bowls. Divide the duck pieces among the bowls, and top with greens, a 1/2 tablespoon each of soy sauce and a tiny drizzle of sesame oil. Pour over the hot stock (do not include the ginger or onions). Serve immediately.

Toasted Noodles
with Vegetables

Serves 4

14 ounces Chinese noodles
1/2 cup pork, sliced
1/4 cup char siu barbecued pork
1/4 cup ham, sliced
2 green onions, chopped
2 tablespoons vegetable oil (for noodles)
2 tablespoons peanut oil (for cooking)
1 clove garlic
1/4 cup thinly shredded carrot
1/2 cup thinly shredded celery
1/2 cup thinly slivered string beans
1/2 cup thinly sliced bamboo shoots
1/2 cup thinly sliced rehydrated dried shiitake mushrooms
1/2 teaspoon salt

Soup Stock
1/2 cup pork, sliced
10 large or 2 tablespoons small dried shrimps
1/3 roll Chinese salted turnip (chung choy)
2-1/2 cups water

Gravy
Soup Stock (above)
1 tablespoon oyster sauce
1 tablespoon soy sauce
1 tablespoon cornstarch
1 teaspoon sugar
1/2 teaspoon rice wine
1/4 teaspoon ginger juice

continued on next page

Seasoning for Pork
1/2 teaspoon soy sauce
1/2 teaspoon sugar
1/2 teaspoon cornstarch

Boil 3 quarts of water in a large pot. Add 1 tablespoon salt and noodles. Boil rapidly for 3 minutes. Drain and wash well in cold water. Drain again and let stand 5 minutes. Mix noodles with oil. Spread noodles thinly on a shallow greased pan and toast in an oven at 450°F until light brown in color.

Make a soup stock by cooking 1/2 cup pork, dried shrimps, salted turnip and water together. Cook at low heat until the liquid reduces to 1-1/2 cups. Strain, combine with gravy ingredients and bring to a boil.

Season 1/2 cup pork with soy sauce, sugar and cornstarch.

Heat 1 tablespoon of peanut oil and pan fry carrots, string beans and bamboo shoots for 2 minutes. Add 2 tablespoons of the gravy and fry 3 minutes longer. Remove from pan and set aside.

Heat remaining 1 tablespoon of peanut oil and add garlic clove and cook until it turns light gold. Add seasoned pork and shiitake mushrooms and pan fry for 2 minutes. Remove garlic; add ham and fry for 1 minute, then add celery and fry for 3 minutes. Return cooked carrots, string beans and bamboo shoots to pan and mix well. Cook for 2 minutes before adding green onion. Turn off flame and place mixture immediately over toasted noodles. Garnish with char siu and cilantro.

Bean Sprout-Scallion Noodles

Serves 6

1/2 pound thin Chinese noodles or angel hair pasta
1-1/2 tablespoons vegetable oil
3 cups finely shredded scallions
3/4 cup finely shredded ginger
1/3 cup Chinese rice wine or sake
3 cups bean sprouts, stringy roots removed
1/4 cup coarsely chopped Chinese parsley

Sauce
1/2 cup chicken broth
1-1/2 tablespoons sesame oil
1-1/2 teaspoons salt or to taste
1/2 teaspoon pepper
1 teaspoon cornstarch

Boil noodles until just tender and drain. Rinse with cold water.

Heat a wok or skillet over high heat. Add the oil and heat for about 30 seconds. Add the scallions and ginger and stir-fry until fragrant, about 20 seconds. Add the rice wine and bean sprouts and toss lightly for about 1 minute, or until well combined.

Add the sesame sauce and the noodles and stir-fry until the sauce thickens, about 2 minutes.

Garnish with Chinese parsley.

Tomato Beef Chow Mein

Serves 4

3 tablespoons oil
3/4 pound Chinese egg noodles
1/2 to 3/4 pound flank steak

Marinade
2 teaspoons cornstarch
2 teaspoons soy sauce
1 tablespoon rice wine or sherry

1 small onion, thinly sliced
2 stalks celery, thinly sliced
2 medium tomatoes, cut into small wedges
1 tablespoon brown sugar
3/4 teaspoon salt

Sauce
1 tablespoon cornstarch
4 tablespoons ketchup
3/4 cup chicken broth
1 tablespoon oyster sauce

Parboil noodles for 3 minutes. Rinse with cold water and drain well. Line cookie sheet with foil and rub with 1 tablespoon of the oil. Put noodles in a thin layer on the cookie sheet. Place in a preheated 400°F oven for 20 minutes. (The noodles will stick together.) Turn noodles over and bake for another 10 minutes. Cool and break into pieces.

continued on next page

Slice beef thinly across the grain and mix with marinade. Allow to soak for 30 minutes. Mix sauce ingredients together and set aside. Sprinkle brown sugar over tomato wedges.

Heat wok or skillet. Add 1/2 tablespoon oil and stir-fry onions and celery for 1-1/2 minutes and season with a little salt. Set aside. Heat remaining 1-1/2 tablespoons oil and stir-fry beef until nearly done, and add tomato wedges to heat through. Set aside.

Pour sauce mixture into same wok or skillet and cook until thickened. Add noodles to sauce and mix until noodles soften. Add salt, vegetables and meat. Mix well and serve immediately.

Gon Lo Mein

Serves 4 to 6

2 tablespoons vegetable oil
1 small onion, thinly sliced
3 stalks celery, de-strung and thinly sliced
1/2 pound char siu, sliced
1 pound Chinese egg noodles
1 package bean sprouts
3 stalks green onion, cut in 1-inch lengths
1 tablespoon sesame seeds

Sauce
2 tablespoons soy sauce
3 tablespoons oyster sauce
1 tablespoon sugar
1 teaspoon salt

Heat oil in large wok or skillet, and stir-fry onion and celery until fragrant. Toss in char siu and cook briefly. Add noodles, bean sprouts and green onion. Stir-fry for 5 minutes. Add sauce and sesame seeds and toss until well combined.

Baked Chow Mein

Serves 4 to 6

1/4 pound char siu, thinly sliced
3/4 pound Chinese egg noodles
1/2 package bean sprouts
1 carrot, julienned
1/4 pound string beans, julienned

Sauce
2 tablespoons soy sauce
3 tablespoons oyster sauce
1 teaspoon garlic powder
1/4 cup peanut oil

Mix all ingredients including sauce in a broiler pan. Bake at
350°F for 20 to 25 minutes.

LONG RICE
(BEAN THREAD NOODLES)

Though they are called "long rice" in Hawai'i, they are
not made with rice at all. Made with mung beans,
these translucent noodles have a slippery texture that
makes them refreshing in salads. These noodles
are also known as "cellophane noodles." Be sure to try
the traditional lū'au dish, Chicken Long Rice.

Chicken Long Rice

Serves 8 to 10 (Recipe may be halved.)

4 packages long rice (bean thread noodles)
5 pounds chicken thighs
1 (2 inch piece) fresh ginger, crushed
3 cloves garlic, crushed
2 onions, quartered
2 to 3 tablespoons vegetable oil
Water and chicken broth
Hawaiian salt and pepper to taste
Instant chicken bouillon powder to taste
1/2 cup green onions, in 1/4-inch pieces

Soak long rice in water to cover. In large skillet, brown chicken thighs on all sides. Stir in ginger, garlic and yellow onions and sauté until chicken is tender. Cool thoroughly, then remove skin and debone. Place meat in refrigerator until needed. Drain long rice and place in large stockpot. Add equal parts of water and chicken broth to cover. Stir in salt and pepper. Simmer until long rice is tender. Add chicken to pot and season to taste with chicken bouillon powder, adding extra chicken broth if more gravy is desired. Garnish with green onions.

Abalone Long Rice Salad

Serves 10

2 packages long rice
1 pound ogo seaweed
4 cucumbers, thinly sliced
1 (15-1/2 ounce) can abalone, thinly sliced

Sauce
1-1/4 cups rice vinegar
3 tablespoons fresh lemon juice
1 cup sugar
1/2 cup soy sauce
4 tablespoons sesame oil
2 tablespoons sesame seeds, toasted and crushed
2 fresh chili peppers, crushed or to taste
2 tablespoons grated fresh ginger

Boil long rice until cooked (about 2 minutes). Drain. Rinse with ice and cold water until chilled. Cut in short lengths. Wash ogo, blanch in boiling water and stir for about 1 minute. Drain and rinse with cold water and cut in short lengths. Marinate noodles and ogo in sauce for 3 hours to overnight. Just before serving, add cucumbers and abalone.

Note: Imitation crab or canned clams may be substituted for abalone.

Thai Long Rice Salad

Serves 8

Long Rice Salad
3 cups long rice (bean thread noodles)
1 cup lettuce, shredded
1 cup cooked, peeled and deveined shrimp
1 cup cooked pork, thinly sliced
2 chili peppers, finely chopped (optional)
2 tablespoons cilantro (Chinese parsley), minced

Dressing
1 tablespoon sugar
2 tablespoons fish sauce
1-1/2 tablespoons lime juice
2 tablespoons Asian chili sauce

Cook long rice according to package directions. Rinse and drain. Mix dressing ingredients together. To serve, arrange noodles with shrimp and pork on a bed of shredded lettuce. Pour dressing on top and garnish with cilantro and chili peppers. Serve immediately.

Kamaboko Long Rice Salad

Serves 4

Long Rice Salad
1 medium won bok (Chinese cabbage)
1 red kamaboko (fish cake), thinly sliced into strips
2 eggs, scrambled, fried in a thin layer and cut into thin strings
1 package (2 ounces) long rice (bean thread noodles)
Long Rice Dressing (see below)

Pour boiling water over long rice in a bowl, and let stand about 20 minutes. Drain in colander and rinse with cold water until cool. Mix in won bok, kamaboko and egg shreds thoroughly and season with dressing. Chill. Salad will keep overnight.

Long Rice Dressing
1/2 cup sugar
1/2 cup vinegar
1/4 cup sesame oil
1/2 cup soy sauce

Combine and mix until sugar is dissolved.

Pancit Miki
Filipino Noodles
Serves 10

This dish uses Japanese udon noodles as well as long rice. Udon are thick wheat noodles that are sold dried in bundles. They may be found at Japanese grocery stores.

1/4 cup achiote seeds
1/2 pound chicken breasts
1/4 pound shrimp, shelled, deveined and cut in 1/2 inch pieces
2 tablespoons vegetable oil
1/2 pound pork, thinly sliced
2 cloves garlic, minced
1 tablespoon fish sauce
3 (14-1/2 ounce) cans chicken broth
1 (9 ounce) package dry udon noodles
1 (4 ounce) package long rice (bean thread noodles), soaked and drained
2 teaspoons salt
1/8 teaspoon pepper
1/4 cup chives, chopped

In a bowl, combine achiote seeds with 1 cup of warm water. Let soak for 30 minutes or longer. Rub seeds with fingers to release red color. Strain through a sieve; discard seeds and reserve achiote water.

continued on next page

Cook chicken in 3 cups of water for 20 minutes. Remove chicken from broth, and reserve broth. Shred chicken.

In a large skillet, heat oil, sauté chicken, shrimp, pork and garlic until pork is no longer pink. Add achiote water, reserved broth and chicken broth. Cover and bring to a boil. Lower heat and simmer for 20 minutes.

In a large pot, boil 10 cups of water, add udon noodles and cook for 10 minutes. Rinse and drain, add to meat mixture with long rice, salt and pepper. Cook for 10 more minutes, stirring frequently. Add chives, and serve immediately.

Long Rice with Pork and Chives

Serves 4

1 bundle long rice (bean thread noodles)
2 cakes tofu
Peanut oil for frying and stir-frying
1/2 cup chives
2 cups bean sprouts
1/2 pound pork
3 green onions, chopped
1 clove garlic, crushed

Seasoning for Pork
1 teaspoon sugar
1 teaspoon soy sauce
1/4 teaspoon ginger juice
1/4 teaspoon rice wine
1/2 teaspoon cornstarch

Gravy
1/2 cup chicken stock
1/2 teaspoon cornstarch
1 teaspoon soy sauce
1/2 teaspoon sugar

continued on next page

Cut tofu into strips about the size of French fried potatoes. Fry slowly in peanut oil until brown.

Discard tips from chives and cut remainder into 1-1/2-inch lengths. Keep bottom and top parts of chives separate, as the lower part (near the root) requires longer cooking. Clean sprouts and remove stringy root ends. Soak long rice for 20 minutes and cut into 3 inch lengths. Cut pork into thin slices and season. Cut green onions into 1-1/2-inch lengths.

Heat 2 teaspoons peanut oil, add crushed clove of garlic and a few pieces of green onion. Add the seasoned pork, add a tablespoon of water, cover the pan and cook for 2 minutes. Remove from the pan.

Heat 2 teaspoons peanut oil, fry the chive bottoms and half the green onions. Cook for 3 minutes, add the tops of the chives and cook for another minute. Add the bean sprouts and the rest of the green onions. Add the long rice and mix thoroughly. Cook for 3 minutes. Add fried tofu strips. Blend ingredients for gravy. Add to long rice, pork and chive mixture. Bring to a boil and serve garnished with cilantro, if desired.

RICE NOODLES
RICE STICKS AND RICE VERMICELLI

Noodles made with rice have a texture somewhere between
that of firm egg noodles and slippery long rice. They
are just as versatile as egg noodles, appearing in stir-fries,
soups and salads. They even may be deep fried to
become delicately puffed and crisp, as you will see if you
try the Crispy Chinese Chicken Salad.
Rice "sticks" appear in a variety of forms: the flat dried type
is used for dishes like Vietnamese Beef Soup and Pad
Thai with Shrimp. Rice vermicelli is the thinner version of
this noodle, and it makes wonderful salads, such as
the Vermicelli Salad with Garlic Shrimp. Chow fun is a soft,
wide noodle sold fresh. All rice noodles may be
found in Hawai'i supermarkets and Asian grocery stores.

Star Anise Beef Noodles

Serves 4 to 6

2 pounds beef chuck, cut into 1-inch cubes

Marinade
2 stalks lemongrass, finely chopped
1 pinch five spice powder
1/4 teaspoon pepper
2 cloves garlic, minced
2 slices ginger, minced
1-1/2 teaspoons Asian chili paste
1 teaspoon salt
1 tablespoon soy sauce
2 teaspoons sugar

1 tablespoon vegetable oil
1 small onion, chopped
2 cloves garlic, minced
2 tablespoons tomato paste
1 teaspoon minced chilies (optional)
1 teaspoon soy sauce
4-1/2 cups water
2 whole star anise pods

1/2 pound rice stick noodles
1/2 cup fresh basil

Combine marinade ingredients in a bowl and add beef. Mix well and set aside for 10 to 15 minutes to marinate.

In a saucepan over high heat, sauté onion and garlic until translucent, then add tomato paste, chili paste and soy sauce and cook for 1 minute. Add the beef and mix well. Pour in the water and add the star anise, and bring to a boil. Reduce heat and simmer, uncovered, for 1-1/2 hours or until beef is very tender.

Just before serving, soften rice noodles in hot water, then boil until just tender. Drain noodles and divide among 4 to 6 bowls. Ladle stew over the noodles and garnish with fresh basil.

Vietnamese Beef Soup *Phō*

Serves 6

Beef Stock

3 pounds beef shin, neck or oxtails
1 tablespoon salt
1 3-inch chunk ginger, not peeled
1 medium onion
2 shallots
4 cloves
6 whole star anise
1-1/2 cinnamon sticks
2 bay leaves
1/2 tablespoon sugar

Noodle Soup

1 pound dried, flat rice noodles
1 pound beef sirloin

Soup Accompaniments

Lime wedges
Bean sprouts
Fresh Thai basil leaves
Chopped fresh chilies
Shredded coriander leaves
Thinly sliced scallions
Asian chili sauce
Fish sauce

continued on next page

Make the Beef Stock: In a large stockpot, cover shin/neck/oxtails with water and bring to a boil. Drain off the water, and cover the meat with 14 cups of fresh water and add the salt. Bring to a boil again.

Stud the onion with the cloves. Using tongs, char the onion, shallots and ginger over a range burner on medium-high heat. Char the vegetables until fragrant. Rinse off the ash and add ginger, shallots and onion to the stock.

Add the star anise, cinnamon sticks, bay leaves and sugar to the stock. When the liquid comes to a boil, reduce the heat to low and simmer for 2-1/2 hours, skimming when necessary. Strain.

Soak the noodles in hot water for 30 minutes. Drain. Cut the sirloin into paper-thin slices. (In order to do this, it helps to freeze the meat slightly to firm it up before cutting.)

In a large pot, bring the stock to a boil. Put a large handful of noodles into a wire strainer and dip it into the boiling stock. Swirl the noodles with chopsticks for about 20 seconds, or until done but still firm. Shake off stock and place noodles in a soup bowl. Repeat with remaining noodles. Divide raw sirloin slices among the bowls, and pour boiling stock into each. (Hot stock will immediately cook beef.)

Serve with accompaniments. Each diner can adjust flavoring or garnish as desired.

Singapore Noodles

Serves 4 to 6

1/4 pound thin, rice-stick noodles (rice vermicelli)
1 pound shrimp, peeled and deveined

Marinade

2 tablespoons rice wine
2 teaspoons minced fresh ginger
1/2 teaspoon sesame oil

3-1/2 tablespoons vegetable oil
2-1/2 cups finely shredded leeks
1-1/2 tablespoons minced fresh ginger
1 cup finely shredded celery
1 cup finely slivered carrots
2 cups bean sprouts, strings removed and rinsed

Sauce

1/4 cup chicken broth or water
2 tablespoons soy sauce
1/2 teaspoon sugar
A few drops chili oil (optional)
1 teaspoon salt
1/2 teaspoon pepper

continued on next page

1-1/2 tablespoons curry powder
1/4 pound char siu barbecued pork, sliced
1/4 cup cilantro

Soften rice vermicelli in hot water for 20 to 25 minutes and drain.

In a bowl, combine the shrimp with the marinade, and toss to coat. Heat half of the oil in a wok or wide skillet over high heat and stir-fry shrimp just until they turn pink. Remove shrimp with slotted spoon and set aside.

In the same pan, add the ginger and leeks and stir until fragrant, and add the remaining vegetables. Stir and cook just until limp, and add shrimp and sauce. Let cook very briefly so flavors combine, and remove to a bowl.

Wipe wok or skillet clean, and heat remaining oil over moderate heat. Add curry powder and stir while heating it until it is fragrant (be careful not to burn curry powder—if you do, remove burnt curry powder and oil and start over). Immediately start adding fistfuls of rice noodles and toss in curry until well combined and heated through. Add shrimp and vegetables with the sauce, and toss until well combined.

Remove from heat and garnish with barbecued pork and cilantro.

Pad Thai with Shrimp

Serves 4

7 ounces dried flat rice noodles
3 tablespoons tamarind pulp
3 tablespoons light brown sugar
2 tablespoons fish sauce
1 teaspoon Asian chili sauce
3-1/2 tablespoons vegetable oil
2 eggs
2 cloves garlic, peeled and minced
6 ounces shrimp, peeled and deveined
2 ounces fried tofu, soaked in hot water, drained, wiped dry
    and diced
Half bunch chives, cut into 2-inch lengths
1/4 cup chopped Chinese salted turnip (chung choi)
1-1/2 cups bean sprouts
Chopped roasted peanuts

Soak noodles in hot water for 15 minutes, or until pliable.
Drain noodles and set aside.

Dissolve tamarind pulp in 1 cup of hot water. Strain through
a sieve into a bowl, pressing pulp through with a spoon.
Discard seeds. Stir sugar, fish sauce and chili sauce into the
tamarind juice and set aside.

continued on next page

Heat 1/2 tablespoon oil in a small skillet, scramble eggs and cook lightly. Set scrambled eggs aside.

Heat remaining 3 tablespoons oil in a large wok or skillet (preferably non-stick). When hot, add garlic. A few seconds later, add shrimp and quickly stir-fry just until barely pink. Add tofu, chives, salted turnip, half the bean sprouts, the noodles, the scrambled eggs and the tamarind mixture, and cook, tossing constantly until the noodles absorb most of the sauce. Garnish each serving with the remaining bean sprouts and peanuts.

—Originally appeared in Saveur *Magazine*

Chow Fun with Barbecued Pork

Makes 2 main course servings or 4 side course servings

14 ounces fresh rice noodles, cut into 1/2-inch wide strips
    if necessary
1/4 cup plus 1 teaspoon peanut oil
3/4 cup chicken stock
2 tablespoons oyster sauce
1 tablespoon soy sauce
2 teaspoons sugar
1 tablespoon Chinese rice wine or sherry
1/4 pound snow peas, strings removed
4 scallions (green onions) cut into 2-inch long julienne
6 ounces char siu (Chinese barbecued pork) thinly sliced
2 teaspoons finely chopped garlic
2 teaspoons finely chopped peeled fresh ginger
1/2 teaspoon cornstarch mixed with 2 teaspoons water
1/2 cup mung bean sprouts
A few drops Asian sesame oil

Separate noodles, then toss with 1 teaspoon peanut oil.

Stir together 1/2 cup stock, oyster sauce, sugar and rice wine.

continued on next page

Heat a wok over high heat and add remaining 1/4 cup peanut oil, swirling to coat evenly, and heat until it just begins to smoke. Stir-fry noodles, tossing frequently, until soft and translucent, 3 to 4 minutes (noodles will stick together). Add snow peas and scallions and stir-fry until snow peas are bright green and crisp-tender, about 1 minute. Add pork, garlic and ginger and stir-fry 1 minute.

Add stock mixture and bring to a boil, stirring, then add remaining 1/4 cup stock. When mixture boils, stir cornstarch mixture and add to wok, then boil, stirring, until sauce is thickened and noodles are well coated, about 30 seconds. Stir in bean sprouts and remove wok from heat. Season with sesame oil and pepper.

Vermicelli Salad with Grilled Pork

Serves 6

Marinade

3 large shallots, peeled and chopped
3 cloves garlic
1 tablespoon sugar
2 tablespoons fish sauce
1/2 teaspoon black pepper
1/8 teaspoon five spice powder
1 tablespoon rice wine or sherry
1 tablespoon vegetable oil

1 pound boneless pork, thinly sliced

1/2 pound dried rice stick noodles (vermicelli)

1-1/2 cups thinly sliced lettuce
2 medium carrots, finely shredded
2 cups bean sprouts, rinsed and drained
1/2 cup coarsely chopped peanuts
3 tablespoons chopped fresh mint leaves

Dressing (see following page)

continued on next page

In a blender, grind shallots, garlic and sugar to make a coarse paste. Stir in remaining marinade ingredients and combine with pork in a bowl. Toss well to coat the meat. Set aside to marinate for 2 hours at room temperature or overnight in the refrigerator.

Soften noodles in hot water, then boil until just tender. Rinse under cold water and drain. Divide lettuce, carrots and bean sprouts among 6 deep bowls and top with noodles.

Grill or broil the pork until brown and crisp around the edges. Decoratively arrange pork slices on the noodles and scatter mint leaves and peanuts over the pork. Serve with Dressing.

Dressing

1 teaspoon dried chili flakes
1/2 tablespoon rice vinegar
1/4 cup fish sauce
2 tablespoons fresh lime juice
1/2 small carrot, finely shredded, rinsed and squeezed dry
1 clove garlic, minced
1/4 cup sugar
3/4 cup warm water

Soak chili flakes in vinegar for about 2 minutes.

In the bowl with the chilies, add the fish sauce, lime juice, carrot, garlic and sugar. Add warm water and stir until sugar is dissolved.

Vermicelli Salad with Garlic Shrimp

Serves 6

This main-course salad is the same as the Vermicelli Salad with Grilled Pork, but with deliciously garlicky shrimp instead of pork.

1/2 pound dried rice-stick noodles (vermicelli)

Garlic Shrimp
1-1/2 tablespoons vegetable oil
8 small cloves garlic, minced
1 pound shrimp, peeled and deveined
1/2 teaspoon pepper
1/2 teaspoon salt
1-1/2 teaspoons sugar
1 teaspoon dried chili flakes
1 large stalk green onion, minced

1-1/2 cups thinly sliced lettuce
2 medium carrots, finely shredded
2 cups bean sprouts, rinsed and drained
1/2 cup coarsely chopped peanuts
3 tablespoons chopped fresh mint leaves

Dressing (See preceding recipe)

continued on next page

Soften noodles in hot water, then boil until just tender. Rinse under cold water and drain.

Make Garlic Shrimp: In a wok or large skillet, heat the oil over medium-high heat. Add the garlic and stir-fry until light gold. Add the shrimp and black pepper and stir-fry until shrimp just turns pink, about 1 minute. Add the salt, sugar and chili flakes and cook for another minute. Toss in the green onion and mix thoroughly.

Divide lettuce, carrots and bean sprouts among 6 deep bowls and top with noodles. Divide shrimp among the bowls and scatter mint leaves and peanuts over the shrimp. Serve with Dressing.

Crispy Chinese Chicken Salad

Serves 6

1 fryer chicken, roasted or boiled
1 head iceberg lettuce
2 tablespoons sesame seeds
4 green onions, sliced in thin, diagonal julienne
1/4 cup chopped peanuts or macadamia nuts
1 package rice sticks (mai fun)
Vegetable oil for frying
Cilantro (Chinese parsley)

Dressing
2 teaspoons salt
1 teaspoon pepper
6 tablespoons vinegar
4 tablespoons sugar
1/3 cup vegetable oil
2 tablespoons sesame oil

Remove meat from chicken and hand-shred into bite-size pieces. Taste and adjust for salt if necessary. Refrigerate until needed. Wash and shred lettuce and toss in large salad bowl with sesame seeds, green onions and nuts. Refrigerate until needed.

continued on next page

Make dressing: Combine dressing ingredients and stir until sugar and salt dissolves.

Pour vegetable oil in pan or deep fryer to a depth of at least 2 inches, and heat to 375° to 400°F. Deep fry rice sticks a little at a time (when rice sticks hit the oil, they will puff up and crisp immediately). Remove rice sticks as they puff, and place in a basket or bowl lined with paper towels to absorb excess oil. Add crisp rice sticks and chicken to the lettuce salad just before serving. Toss salad with dressing and garnish with cilantro.

SOBA
BUCKWHEAT NOODLES

SOMEN
THIN WHEAT NOODLES

Hawai'i's large Japanese population enjoys the hearty taste of buckwheat in healthful soba noodles. As the weather is always warm in the Islands, Japanese somen noodles have also become very popular, as they are traditionally eaten cold in the summer. Somen Salad is a dish often seen at local potluck parties.

Zaru Soba *Chilled Buckwheat Noodles*

Serves 4

The Japanese name for this dish means "basket noodles," as the noodles are customarily served in baskets or boxes with slatted bottoms so the water drains out. You can buy the traditional serving dishes at Japanese stores, but ordinary plates may also be used, so long as the noodles are drained well.

1/2 pound dried buckwheat noodles (soba)
3 cups bottled soba dipping sauce (soba tsuyu), or see **Soba Tsuyu** recipe on next page
2 sheets nori

Condiments

1 teaspoon wasabi, or more to taste
5 tablespoons finely chopped green onion
4 tablespoons finely grated daikon (optional)

Boil noodles in plenty of water, following package directions. Drain noodles into a colander, rinse well with cold water to remove excess starch, and add ice cubes and toss well to chill. Remove ice cubes and drain well. Divide among 4 baskets or plates.

Follow directions on bottle of soba tsuyu to make 3 cups, or make Soba Tsuyu recipe below. In four small, deep bowls, pour about 1/2 cup of tsuyu each. Pour rest of the tsuyu into a small pitcher.

Crisp nori sheets one at a time over a range burner, and use a pair of scissors to cut nori into fine shreds. Sprinkle nori shreds in the center of each pile of noodles.

Divide condiments among 4 small dishes, piling them in separate mounds. Each table setting would have a noodle basket, a tsuyu bowl, a small dish of condiments and a pair of chopsticks.

Each diner should be instructed to mix desired condiments into the sauce, dip the noodles into the tsuyu and eat. Keep the small pitcher of the extra tsuyu on the side in case anyone runs out.

Soba Tsuyu
2-1/2 cups water
1/2 cup plus 2 tablespoons soy sauce
4 tablespoons mirin
1 teaspoon sugar
3 cups, loosely packed hana katsuo (dried bonito flakes)

In a medium saucepan, mix all ingredients except hana katsuo and heat just to a boil. Stir in hana katsuo and immediately remove from heat. Wait for about 10 seconds, or until flakes settle, and strain. Let cool to room temperature and chill. If it is to be used immediately, put liquid into a metal bowl and swirl bowl in a larger bowl filled with ice and water until tsuyu is chilled.

Chicken and Green Onion Soba Soup

Serves 4

Broth

4 cups **Dashi** (see recipe on next page)
1 teaspoon salt
3 tablespoons soy sauce
1 tablespoon sugar
1 tablespoon mirin

Chicken and Marinade

1 pound boneless and skinless chicken meat, cut in slices
3-1/2 tablespoons soy sauce
1-1/2 tablespoons rice wine or sherry
1 tablespoon minced ginger

1 pound dried soba noodles
6 to 8 green onions sliced on diagonal

Combine ingredients for broth.

Marinate chicken pieces in ginger marinade for 15 minutes.

Boil soba noodles as directed on package and drain. Divide the noodles among 4 soup bowls.

Bring broth to a gentle boil. Drain marinade off of chicken, and add chicken pieces to broth. Simmer for about 5 minutes, or until tender. Skim the broth surface as needed. Add green onions and simmer for 1 minute more.

Ladle broth over each portion, and arrange chicken pieces and green onion slices over noodles. Serve immediately.

Dashi

4 cups cold water
1 ounce kelp (dashi kombu)
1 ounce hana katsuo flakes

Fill a medium sized pot with the water and put in the kelp. Heat, uncovered, on medium-high flame so as to reach the boiling point in about 10 minutes. Do not allow kelp to boil, as it will release a nasty flavor. Be sure to remove kelp before water boils.

Test kelp by piercing it with your thumbnail. If it is soft, then it has flavored the broth sufficiently. If it's still hard, put 1/4 cup of cold water into the pot to lower the stock's temperature and put the kelp back in for a minute or two.

After removing the kelp, bring the stock to a full boil. Add 1/4 cup cold water and immediately add the hana katsuo flakes. Bring to a full boil, and immediately remove the pot from heat. (If boiled too long, the stock will be too strong.)

Allow the hana katsuo flakes to start to settle to the bottom of the pot (about 30 seconds to 1 minute) and filter through a cheesecloth-lined sieve.

A Note on the Ingredients
You can find the dashi kombu and hana katsuo at Japanese grocery stores. Be sure to get the thicker dashi kelp rather than the type used for stewing. Hana katsuo is normally sold in clear plastic packets, and the flakes resemble wood shavings from a plane. These shavings are cut from a specially cured aku (katsuo in Japanese), and have a pleasant smoky flavor.

Cold Somen in Soup

Serves 6

1 large daikon turnip
7 teaspoons salt
1 red chili pepper, seeded and minced
1 clove garlic, minced
1 teaspoon minced ginger root
2 tablespoons chopped green onions
1 teaspoon sugar
12 cups water
1 package (9 ounces) somen noodles
4 cups instant dashi (or make **Dashi**, see recipe on p. 60)

Pare turnip and cut into 1/4-inch slices. Rub 3 teaspoons of the salt into turnip, let stand 15 minutes and rinse. Combine 2 more teaspoons of the salt with the chili, garlic, ginger, green onion, 6 cups of water and 1/2 teaspoon of the sugar and add the turnip. Refrigerate for at least 2 days.

Boil somen in 6 cups of water, drain and chill with ice cubes and cold water. Drain well. Drain brine from turnip and reserve both brine and turnip. Divide somen among 6 soup bowls. Combine the reserved brine with instant dashi, the remaining 2 teaspoons salt and 1/2 teaspoon sugar. Pour soup over somen and serve the turnip slices on the somen.

Gingered Scallops with Colorful Soba Noodles

Serves 6

This soba salad has beautiful vegetable colors—carrot curls, zucchini curls, red bell pepper strips, plus scallops poached in ginger stock.

1-1/2 pounds scallops
2 teaspoons canola oil

Marinade:
1-1/2 tablespoons dry white wine
1-1/2 tablespoons orange juice
1 tablespoon minced ginger
1 tablespoon minced red bell pepper (or 1 Hawaiian red chile
    pepper, seeded and minced)
1 tablespoon minced yellow bell pepper
1 tablespoon chopped fresh basil
1 tablespoon minced cilantro
1/2 teaspoon sugar
Salt and white pepper to taste

Pasta Mixture:
1/2 pound soba (Japanese thin brown wheat noodles)
12 fresh spinach leaves
1/2 cup julienned carrots
1/2 cup julienned red bell pepper
1/2 cup julienned zucchini
12 fresh basil leaves
1 tablespoon minced cilantro
1 tablespoon soy sauce
1 tablespoon olive oil
1 teaspoon sesame seed oil
1 teaspoon minced garlic

continued on next page

In a bowl, combine marinade ingredients and marinate scallops.

Cook soba according to package directions; drain. In a large mixing bowl, combine soba with remaining pasta-mixture ingredients. Toss like a Caesar salad.

In a skillet, heat oil over medium heat and sauté scallops 1-1/2 minutes on each side; do not overcook. Pour scallops and juices right over soba.

—*Originally appeared in* The Choy of Cooking

PASTA

Though Hawai'i doesn't have a large Italian population, local cooks have created their own favorites. The noodle casserole is well loved among busy home cooks, and two versions are in this section to enjoy. Hawai'i's chefs have taken pastas and transformed them into unique Island-accented dishes. Three fabulous dishes by chef Sam Choy are featured here.

Chinese Pasta with Sesame-Crusted Opah

Serves 4

This recipe combines the rich taste of perfectly cooked opah with a light, and fresh bed of flash-cooked vegetables and pasta. The culinary balance will satisfy every palate. Sit back, and wait for the compliments from your dinner guests.

1 pound linguine or your favorite pasta
1 tablespoon light olive oil
1 tablespoon butter
1 clove fresh garlic, minced
1 medium red bell pepper, cut in strips
1 carrot, cut into thin strips
2 medium zucchinis, trimmed but not peeled, sliced
1/2 pound fresh broccoli florets
1/2 pound fresh asparagus, cut in 1 inch pieces
1/2 pound whole sugar snap peas
6 green onions, sliced thin
2 tablespoons fresh Thai basil
1/4 cup fresh cilantro, chopped
1 tablespoon Aloha shoyu
Salt and pepper to taste
1/4 cup Parmesan cheese
Sesame-Crusted Opah (see recipe on next page)

Cook pasta according to directions on the package.

Meanwhile, heat the oil and butter in a wok. Add the garlic, then all the vegetables, toss and cook 1 to 2 minutes. Add basil, cilantro, shoyu, salt, and pepper. Cook 1 minute more. Add linguine and Parmesan cheese to vegetable mixture, and

continued on next page

toss. Serve on warm platter. Top with Sesame-Crusted Opah.

Sesame-Crusted Opah
4 opah fillets, 6 ounces each
1 large egg, beaten
1/4 cup black goma (black sesame seeds)
1/4 cup while sesame seeds
1/4 cup salad oil
Salt and pepper to taste

Season fish with salt and pepper. Mix black goma and white sesame seeds. Dip fish into beaten eggs, then coat with sesame seeds. Heat oil in skillet, and sauté fish for 2 to 3 minutes on each side until golden brown.

Opah don't travel in schools. Individual fish are harvested by longline fleets anchored over seamounts where the opah congregate. Opah have no set migratory pattern, but fishermen believe that they move vertically up the steep slopes of seamounts in search of food. In Island waters there is a good year-round supply of opah with peak quantities caught during the months between April and August.

—*Originally appeared in* The Choy of Seafood

Easy Macaroni Casserole

Serves 4

2 small green peppers, thinly sliced
2 tablespoons vegetable oil
1 large onion, chopped
1 pound ground beef
Salt and pepper to taste
3 cups tomato juice
1 teaspoon Worcestershire sauce
2 cups uncooked macaroni

In a large heavy skillet or pot, sauté peppers in oil until softened. Add onion and sauté until transparent. Add ground beef, salt and pepper to taste and cook until browned. Add tomato juice, Worcestershire sauce and macaroni. Bring to a boil, lower heat and simmer for 30 minutes.

Oriental Lamb Chops with Rotelli Pasta

Serves 4 to 6

I've been very blessed with this dish being so successful in our restaurant. Basically, I've taken Chinese methods and flavorings, added a twist, and come up with this award-winning recipe.

2 or 3 lamb chops per serving (8 to 18 chops total)

Marinade:
1/2 cup shoyu
3/4 cup garlic, minced
1 Tbsp. fresh ginger, minced
2 cups brown sugar
1/2 tsp. chili flakes
1/2 cup basil, minced
1/2 cup Chinese parsley, minced
Salt to taste

Combine marinade ingredients, massage into meat for 5 to 10 minutes, then let marinate 4 to 6 hours in refrigerator.

Broil to perfection (about 2 to 3 minutes per side for medium rare, or to your liking.)

Rotelli Pasta:
2 Tbsp. butter
4 Tbsp. olive oil
1-1/2 Tbsp. garlic, minced
1 medium carrot, julienned
2 medium zucchini, julienned
2 cups shiitake mushrooms, julienned
1/2 cup Chinese parsley, coarsely chopped

continued on next page

12 oz. bag rotelli, cooked according to package
        directions, drained
6 cups heavy cream
Salt and pepper to taste
3/4 cup grated Parmesan cheese

In a large saucepan, heat butter and olive oil over medium-high heat, cook garlic for about 1 minute, without browning, then add vegetables and stir-fry for 2 to 3 minutes. Add drained cooked pasta and stir-fry another minute. Add heavy cream, bring to a boil, then immediately reduce to a simmer. Adjust seasoning with salt and pepper. Just before serving fold in 3/4 cup Parmesan cheese and let cook 1 minute.

Serve in large pasta bowls with 2 or 3 *Oriental Lamb Chops* on top, garnish with sprigs of fresh basil.

—*Originally appeared in* With Sam Choy

Crab Potato Pasta Salad

Serves 6

8 ounces elbow macaroni or other similar pasta, cooked
5 or 6 hard-cooked eggs, chopped
3 large potatoes, boiled and diced
1 pint (16 ounces) mayonnaise
1 pound crab meat or 1 tray imitation crab, shredded
1/2 cup diced celery
1/2 cup grated carrots
1/2 cup frozen peas, defrosted and drained
5 or 6 black olives, chopped
Salt and pepper to taste

Mix all ingredients. Chill well before serving.

Chinese Pasta Primavera

Serves 8

This is my way of blending both Chinese and Italian influences in a hearty pasta dish.

1 lb. linguine
1 medium red bell pepper, cut in strips
1 medium yellow bell pepper, cut in strips
2 medium zucchini, trimmed but not peeled, sliced
1/2 lb. broccoli florets
1/2 lb. fresh asparagus, cut in 1-inch pieces
1/2 lb. whole sugar snap peas, or Chinese snow peas
6 shallots or green onions, sliced thin
1 clove garlic, minced
1 Tbsp. butter
1 Tbsp. olive oil
1/4 cup Chinese parsley, chopped
2 Tbsp. Thai basil
1 Tbsp. shoyu
Salt and pepper to taste
1/4 cup Parmesan cheese, freshly grated

Fill a large pot with water and begin heating it for the pasta. Heat oil and butter in a large skillet or wok and stir-fry vegetables, onions, and garlic about 3 minutes. Add parsley and basil and cook another minute, or until vegetables are done to your taste – they should be a little crunchy.

When water boils, add linguine and cook according to package directions; it should be al dente. Season vegetables with salt and pepper, mix with shoyu, toss with pasta, and sprinkle with Parmesan.

continued on next page

Pasta is a very interesting dish. It is a trendy food of the 90s, while at the same time it is one of those classics that will never change. People like it, and it's healthy, simple, and satisfying. It's just water, salt, and flour, and sometimes eggs, and you can't get more basic than that. When Marco Polo toured China, he fell in love with noodles and brought the concept back to Italy. But when the Italians tried to make Chinese noodles, they had to use the flour and methods available in Italy, which were very different from those in China, and that's why Italian pasta is different from Chinese. But it's the same basic idea.

—*Originally appeared in* With Sam Choy

Noodle Glossary

A

Achiote seeds:
the seeds of the annatto plant, which lend a red color and a flavor a bit like green olives to Filipino dishes. Also called annatto seeds.

Ao nori:
green flakes of dried seaweed used as a flavoring. This may be found in Japanese grocery stores.

Asian chili sauce:
this type of sauce is composed of chili peppers, garlic, salt and sugar. Sriracha sauce is an example.

B

Bean thread noodles:
a thin, clear noodle made from the starch of the mung bean. These relatively flavorless noodles soak up the flavors of other ingredients in a dish. They are also called cellophane noodles, and are known as long rice in Hawai'i.

C

Char siu:
a Chinese version of barbecued pork, usually colored red and sweet in flavor.

Chili paste:
a condiment composed of hot red chilies, vinegar, salt and sometimes garlic. Indonesian or Malay Sambal Oelek is an example.

Chinese cabbage:
also known as celery cabbage, Chinese cabbage and won bok. Pale green at the top to white at the stem with crinkly leaves.

Cilantro:
leaves of the coriander plant. Also known as Chinese parsley.

D

Dashi:
the basic stock for Japanese soups and sauces, made from HANA KATSUO and DASHI KOMBU. See Recipe, p. 60.

Dashi kombu:
deep olive-green dried kelp of species *Laminaria*. Kombu (the name for kelp generically) is used for making soup stock and eaten as a vegetable. Dashi kombu is specifically the type used for making DASHI.

F

Fish sauce:
  a thin, brown and salty liquid made from salted anchovies. Vietnam, Thailand and the Philippines produce this condiment, where it is used much like soy sauce is used in Japan or China.

Five spice powder:
  a spice blend generally consisting of ground cloves, fennel seeds, star anise, cinnamon and Szechwan pepper; used in Chinese and Vietnamese cuisines.

G

Ginger:
  the gnarled rhizome of a tall, flowering plant (*Zingiber officinale*) native to China. In Hawai'i, where it is grown, it is most frequently used fresh. Though also available powdered, pickled or candied, these forms are not good substitutes for fresh ginger.

H

Hana katsuo:
  shavings of KATSUOBUSHI (dried preserved aku) used for making DASHI stock. These can be purchased pre-packaged at Japanese grocery stores.

Hawaiian salt:
  coarse sea salt.

J

Julienne:
  to cut a food into thin strips similar in size to matchsticks.

K

Katsuobushi:
  steamed and dried filets of aku as hard as wood. These preserved filets have a long history—aku have been preserved this way in Japan since the fifteenth century. The katsuobushi are shaved into flakes with the use of a tool similar to a wood plane. Though the katsuobushi themselves are difficult to purchase outside of Japan, the shavings, called HANA KATSUO, are fairly easily obtainable. The flakes are used in making DASHI stock and as a condiment.

L

Long rice:
  translucent thread-like noodles made from mung bean flour. See BEAN THREAD NOODLES.

78

M

Macadamia nuts:
    rich, slightly sweet nuts that
    are a major crop in Hawai'i; often
    called "Mac Nuts."

N

Nori:
    dark green, purple or black sheets
    of dried seaweed with a slightly
    briny flavor. Sheets are paper-thin
    and may be flavored with soy
    sauce and sugar. This type of nori
    is called Ajitsuke Nori. The
    unflavored plain version is what is
    used for Sushi.

O

Oyster sauce:
    a concentrated dark-brown sauce
    made from oysters, salt and soy
    sauce. Used in many Asian dishes
    to impart a full, rich flavor.

R

Rice vinegar:
    a type of vinegar made from rice
    wine; generally clear with a pale
    straw color. Generally, rice vinegar
    is mellow and lower in acid than
    other vinegars.

S

Sesame oil:
    oil pressed from the sesame seed
    is available in two forms. Pressing
    the raw seed produces an oil
    which is light in color and flavor
    and can be used for a wide variety
    of purposes. When the oil is
    pressed from toasted sesame
    seeds, it is dark in color with a
    much stronger flavor. It is this
    darker version that is to be used
    in the recipes in this book.

Sesame seeds:
    the edible seeds of a plant of the
    Pedaliaceae family that have a
    distinctive nutty flavor. They come
    in black or white varieties, and are
    known as benne seeds and goma.

Shallot:
    this member of the onion family
    forms a bulb more like a garlic
    bulb and has a subtler flavor than
    green onions.

Shiitake mushrooms:
    mushrooms native to Japan that
    are now cultivated in the Untied
    States; have tough stems that are
    not eaten and dark brown caps
    that have a meaty, smoky flavor.
    Dried shiitake need to be soaked
    in warm water until soft (20 to 30
    minutes). Also called black
    Chinese mushrooms and golden
    oak mushrooms.

Snow peas:
    young peas with edible pods consumed when the pods are thin and the seeds are still tiny.

Soy sauce:
    a sauce made from fermented boiled soybeans and roasted wheat or barley; its color ranges from light or dark brown and its flavor is generally rich and salty. Used extensively in Chinese and Japanese cuisines as a flavoring, condiment and a cooking medium.

Star anise:
    the dried star-shaped fruit of the Chinese magnolia. Used for their strong licorice fragrance.

T

Tamarind pulp:
    the dark brown dried pulp of a fruit that has an intriguing sour flavor recognizable from Worcestershire sauce. Tamarind pulp is sold in blocks at Asian grocery stores.

Tofu:
    Japanese name for a bland soy bean curd that can be custard-like in texture or quite firm. The firm or extra firm varieties are generally used in stir-frying or deep-frying.

W

Wasabi:
    also called Japanese horseradish; comes in both powder and paste forms. It is pale green in color, and produces a sharp, tingling sensation in the nose and palate.

Wok:
    a round or flat-bottomed Chinese cooking pan used for stir-frying or deep-frying foods.

Z

Zest:
    the colored portion of a citrus fruit's rind. When removing the zest from a citrus fruit, it's important to avoid removing the bitter white pith just below the colored portion.